Let Them Fly

Other books in the Wisdom & Warnings series

From Divorce Mess to Happiness

The Badass Woman

Tips from the Quad

Because You Care

Happily Ever After

Our library of wisdom keeps growing!
Check out the full list anytime at wisdomandwarnings.com or
simply scan the QR code.

Let Them Fly

100 Tips to Let Your New College Student Soar and Rediscover Yourself

Jen Fort

From the Wisdom & Warnings®
book series

Disclaimer

The author of *Let Them Fly* is not a licensed therapist. Because of this, this book is presented solely for educational and entertainment purposes and is not intended to be a substitute for the advice of a physician, professional coach, therapist, and other qualified professionals.

This book was created with the assistance of various resources, including AI as a brainstorming tool to help organize ideas and enhance clarity. However, all insights, concepts, and creative content are entirely the author's.

Let Them Fly

100 Tips to Let Your New College Student Soar and Rediscover Yourself

Jen Fort

From the Wisdom & Warnings®
book series

Disclaimer

The author of *Let Them Fly* is not a licensed therapist. Because of this, this book is presented solely for educational and entertainment purposes and is not intended to be a substitute for the advice of a physician, professional coach, therapist, and other qualified professionals.

This book was created with the assistance of various resources, including AI as a brainstorming tool to help organize ideas and enhance clarity. However, all insights, concepts, and creative content are entirely the author's.

Dedication

This book is dedicated to every parent who poured their heart into raising strong, confident, capable children—and had the courage to let them soar.

Share Your Wisdom!

Wisdom & Warnings consists of nearly 8,000 carefully curated nuggets of wisdom on dozens of topics related to life's milestones, ranging from relationships to parents/children to education and career, plus fun topics for living your best life.

Engage with the Wisdom & Warnings community for ongoing encouragement through life's milestones.

www.wisdomandwarnings.com
Facebook: https://www.facebook.com/wisdomandwarnings/
Instagram: @wisdomandwarnings
Email: hello@wisdomandwarnings.com

Table of Contents

My Story

There's something magical about hearing the right words at just the right time—a spark of wisdom that can brighten a day, guide a decision, or even change the course of a life. I've always been drawn to those small but powerful truths. From an early age, I found myself captivated by people's stories—their struggles, triumphs, and the nuggets of wisdom they carried. Every person I met seemed to have something unique to teach me, and I couldn't help but ask: *What's your lesson?*

That curiosity became the seed of a passion I call *Wisdom & Warnings*—a lifelong quest to learn from the experiences of others. Over the years, I turned conversations into a collection of insights. Friends, family, and even strangers shared their advice with me, often without realizing how profound their words were. By the time I looked back, I had gathered over 8,000 pieces of advice—a treasure chest of wisdom just waiting to be shared. But for the longest time, I didn't.

Self-doubt became my shadow. *What if I fail? What if no one cares?* Those questions kept me in a cycle of "someday" and "not yet." I tinkered with the idea for over a decade, hesitating to commit fully. Deep down, though, I couldn't shake the feeling that this treasure wasn't meant to stay hidden. Whenever I thought about shelving the project, a little voice whispered, "Life is too short not to learn from each other." It felt selfish not sharing, but fear has a way of making even the best ideas feel impossible.

*Fear, my friends, is a topic for another time.

Then, life gave me an unexpected push. I lost my job—a moment that felt devastating at first but turned out to be the break I needed. Suddenly, I had time to reflect, and one thing became crystal clear: it was now or never. Those whispers urging me to share my collection became impossible to ignore. I realized that I didn't need to be perfect or polished; I just needed to start.

So, I took a leap of faith with no formal writing experience and zero understanding of the publishing world. That leap became the *365 Days of Wisdom & Warnings* book series. Along the way, I've made mistakes, learned lessons, and celebrated every small victory. More than anything, I've realized that when you listen to the quiet whispers of your heart, you're led to something greater than fear: purpose.

If this journey has taught me anything, it's that the world needs what only you can offer. You might feel unqualified or unsure, but someone out there is waiting for what you have to give. My wish for you is this: trust those quiet whispers, silence the doubts—whether they're yours or someone else's—and chase what sets your soul on fire. Your passion could be the light that sparks someone else's journey. And isn't that the real magic?

I'll be cheering you on.

Jen

Introduction

Sending your child off to college is a bittersweet milestone. As a parent, you've spent years nurturing, guiding, and preparing them for this moment. Now, as they stand on the brink of independence, you may feel a mix of pride, anxiety, and sadness. But take heart—this transition is what you've been working toward all along.

Letting go isn't easy, and it's natural to worry, but your support as a parent doesn't end; it simply evolves. You're still their anchor, but now it's time to let them take charge of their journey, even as they stumble and learn. This is how they'll develop resilience, problem-solving skills, and confidence in their abilities.

So, take a deep breath. It's okay to feel emotional but remember this: the foundation you've laid for your child is solid. They have everything they need within themselves to succeed. Your task now is to let go with grace and positivity, knowing that this is their time to fly. Be proud of how far they've come, and trust that you've given them the resources to thrive.

This book is a culmination of wisdom from parents who have been exactly where you are now. On each page you will see a bit of the conversation which inspired the day's wisdom. While I don't recall names, this is my way of honoring the wisdom-giver by including their perspective. They've faced the same doubts, joys, and growing pains and shared the lessons they've learned to make the transition smoother for both parent and child. From their practical tips to emotional insights, these pages will guide you through this shift.

Your job as a parent isn't finished—it's just evolving!

Chapter 1

Countdown to Campus:
Essential Skills to Teach Before They Fly Solo

#1

Enjoy the little moments while your child is still at home.

The hustle and bustle of daily life can make it easy to overlook the small, quiet moments you'll miss when they're away. Whether it's sharing a cup of coffee in the morning, having a spontaneous chat about their day, or watching a favorite TV show together, these moments are the building blocks of memories. As they prepare to leave for college, the routine of everyday life might feel like it's taking a backseat to all the big decisions and preparations. But it's these simple, everyday interactions that really matter. Take time to savor the laughter, the inside jokes, and the comfort of just being in the same space. You'll never get this exact version of them again, and before you know it, they'll be off starting their own adventures. When they leave, these little moments will be the ones that stick with you.

> *"I stopped nagging my son about playing video games and grabbed a controller instead. Turns out, those gaming sessions became some of my favorite moments."*

#2

Be super clear about how much out-of-pocket expense you can afford... then tell your child.

Even if you can, you are not required to shoulder 100% of your child's higher education costs. Students who contribute to their tuition are more likely to take college seriously. Start early by determining how much of the expense you can afford and have an honest conversation with your child. This discussion can guide them toward choosing a local school instead of one across the country. You might decide to pay for tuition while your child covers books and housing. Or, you could agree to pay the cost of a local school, leaving your child responsible for the difference if they opt for an out-of-state or more prestigious school. Another option is to split the costs. Encourage your child to explore scholarships, grants, and financial aid options. Help them understand the importance of budgeting and planning for college expenses but let them do the legwork. Guide them in researching work-study opportunities, payment plans, and student loans, but give them the responsibility of understanding what's needed. This conversation isn't easy, but it's necessary to avoid the stress of overspending and to help your child understand the importance of budgeting and financial planning... so you don't end up being their personal ATM.

"As a single parent, I had to get creative with how to pay for our daughter's college education. Ultimately, tuition would be split three ways: me, her father, and my daughter."

#3

Tour schools with your child but let them take the lead.

This is your child's journey, and while you can offer guidance and support, the decision about where they feel most comfortable should come from them. When you visit campuses, encourage them to ask questions, talk to current students, and explore the areas that matter most to them, whether it's academic buildings, dorms, or social spaces. Let them feel the vibe of each campus and see where they feel most at home. You can give input or share your observations but avoid pushing them toward a particular choice. This is about helping them learn what's important to them, whether it's location, campus culture, or specific programs. By letting them take charge of the tour, you're empowering them to make a decision that feels right for their future. It's also an excellent opportunity to start developing the independence they'll need for college life. Trust that their instincts will guide them and offer a supportive, non-pressuring presence as they figure out where they can thrive.

"Before visiting a campus, I gave my son a campus map and suggested, since we didn't have a ton of time, to circle the areas he most wanted to see. He put dorms, gym, and dining hall at the top of his list; then I got to add a few of my own, like the library. By letting him set priorities, he felt in control, and I still made sure other must-do's were covered."

#4

Come up with a mutually agreed-upon schedule for staying connected.

Life will get busy for them with classes, socializing, and adjusting to a new routine, so setting regular time for a check-in ensures you're prioritizing communication. It doesn't need to be a long conversation—just a quick call or text to say, "I'm doing okay," and hear about how they're adjusting. You can even sprinkle in some fun by calling it a "Proof of Life call." This small act will help you stay connected without feeling overbearing, giving your child the space to manage their new independence while knowing they have your support. This isn't about obligation, rather it shows that you value the relationship enough to prioritize it. Be realistic and flexible, because life happens and sometimes plans need to be adjusted. Agreeing on a schedule eliminates guesswork and avoids feelings of neglect or pressure.

"Thinking it would be fun, we came up with a 5-star system. Five stars for the most excellent day, three stars for okay, but nothing special, and one star for a very bad day. We realized pretty quick the system was creating anxiety for us parents, so we switched to text messages during the week and a Facetime call on Sunday evening."

#5

Set up a medical power of attorney to access their information if they're hospitalized after turning eighteen.

Once your child turns eighteen, they are legally considered an adult, and you no longer have automatic access to their medical records or decisions. The medical power of attorney allows you to make health-related decisions for them if they cannot do so themselves, whether it's due to an emergency, an illness, or an accident. It's an important step in ensuring that you can step in and advocate for their care when needed, without delays or complications. Having this in place gives both you and your child peace of mind, knowing that, should the unexpected happen, you can help make informed decisions and communicate with healthcare providers without delay. It's a simple yet essential form to fill out, and it ensures that, despite your child's growing independence, you'll still be able to support them when it counts the most.

"I never thought twice about my college kid's medical decisions—until I had to. My 19-year-old son was suddenly hospitalized, unable to speak for himself, and there I was, drowning in paperwork instead of just being there for him. I always assumed I'd have a say, but once they turn 18, it's a whole different ballgame."

#6

Don't let your stress have a negative effect on your child.

When you let stress take over, your child absorbs that tension and can feel unsettled or anxious. They watch you, learn from you, and pick up on your energy—whether you speak about it or not. Instead of letting stress control you, show your child how to handle it with grace. It's not about being perfect but about demonstrating resilience and calmness under pressure. When you manage your stress well, you teach your child that difficult moments don't have to define us. Take a moment to breathe, focus on what you can control, and model healthy ways to cope—whether taking a walk, journaling, or simply talking through your feelings. Encourage your child to do the same, letting them know it's okay to feel stressed, but handling it in a positive way is important. Show them how self-care, open communication, and taking breaks are powerful tools.

"Out of nowhere, my daughter started talking about staying home instead of going to her dream school. I couldn't understand why until she finally admitted she overheard me telling a friend how sad I was about her being so far away. I had no idea she was worrying; to the point where she felt like she couldn't leave. It was a wake-up call for sure."

#7

Offer support with preparation as needed, but let your child take full responsibility for their life at college.

The months leading up to college are a great time to guide them through logistics. Help them with the application process, research housing, and teach them how to manage their finances, but once they step onto that campus, it's their turn to step up. College demands that students manage their time, keep up with coursework, balance social life, and handle the small day-to-day decisions that come with independence. Be there for encouragement, advice, and a listening ear, but let them carry the responsibility. This approach builds both confidence and resilience, while also preparing them for life after college. Children who fully own their college experience are more prepared for the challenges ahead and develop essential skills that will last a lifetime.

> *"I knew that once I dropped my daughter off, my role would be drastically different. So, I made the most of every moment while we shopped and packed. I let her pick the dorm décor, laughed through the 'do you really need that?' debates, and just soaked it all in."*

#8

Plan lunch, dinner, or just a walk around the block and have a meaningful conversation about this next chapter.

It's easy to assume that your child is completely excited and ready for the transition to college, but they might be just as nervous as you. Having an open, honest conversation can allow both of you to express your feelings and share your concerns. It's an excellent opportunity to reassure each other, talk about expectations, and acknowledge that while this is a significant change, it's also a positive one for both of you. You might find that your child has worries or anxieties they haven't voiced yet, and this will give them a safe space to share. At the same time, you can express your support and excitement for their future, reminding them that this new chapter is full of opportunities.

"My son used to be on dish duty after supper, but in the weeks leading up to him leaving for college, I told him I'd handle the dirty dishes after we went for a walk around the block together. It turned into a win-win-win. He got out of scrubbing pots and pans, I got fifteen minutes alone with my son, and the dog was a happy camper."

#9

Go with your child to every Admitted Student Day.

Attending Admitted Student Day with your child is a fantastic way to support them in choosing where to go to college—with emphasis on *them,* not you! These events offer a firsthand look at campus life, and it's essential to focus on what your child observes, feels, and values, rather than steering them toward what you think is best. Let them lead the way—encourage them to ask questions, sit in on presentations, and picture themselves as part of the community. Your role is to support, not decide. Watch how they respond to the vibe of the campus, the students they meet, and the opportunities presented. Afterward, have a judgment-free conversation about what they liked and what didn't feel right. Resist the urge to inject your preferences—this decision sets the tone for their future, and they need to feel ownership. By being a sounding board instead of the decision-maker, you help them build confidence in their choice and feel good about the path they're taking.

> *"Admitted Student Day was a real eye-opener for my son since he didn't get a chance to tour campus before applying. I casually mentioned to be prepared that his dream school on paper might not live up to the hype once he got on campus. I also said it was perfectly fine to change his mind if something didn't feel right. Bingo! The vibe was off, my son changed his mind and ended up at the perfect school... which happened to be last on his list. Funny how things work out."*

#10

Teach your child how to scrub a toilet and clean a shower.

It might not be the flashiest life lesson, but it's one that'll save them—and their roommates—a world of conflict. College life often means shared bathrooms, and knowing how to clean up after themselves isn't just practical—it's a sign of respect (and keeps everyone happier). Teach them the basics: how to tackle all of the nooks and crannies in a bathroom. Keep it simple—show them a quick routine they can stick to, whether it's once a week or when things start looking scary. It may seem trivial, but this little habit builds independence, keeps the peace in shared spaces, and makes their living situation healthier and less stressful. Hopefully they'll continue those cleaning habits long after their college days are over and perhaps even if they return home!

> *"It floored me that my daughter's roommates had no clue how to clean a toilet! I ended up giving toilet cleaning tutorials on move-in day. It was totally embarrassing for my daughter, but as a mom, you gotta do what you gotta do!"*

#11

Ask them: "What are you most looking forward to once you get to college?"

This simple question opens a conversation focusing on their excitement and anticipation for this next significant chapter. College is a time of new experiences, and your child is feeling nervous and excited about the opportunities ahead. By asking this question, you allow them to express what they're most excited about, such as meeting new people, discovering their passions, or getting involved in campus activities. It also provides insight into their mindset, helping you understand their emotional and mental state. The conversation shifts from potential worries to the many possibilities, allowing both of you to focus on the exciting journey that college represents. Understanding what excites them can also give you the opportunity to talk about how to balance freedom with responsibility, plus, showing genuine interest in their hopes and dreams strengthens your connection and supports their independence as they prepare to step into this new phase of life.

"When I asked my daughter what she was looking forward to, the conversation started out great, but then I got excited and started over-sharing my own experience. My daughter quickly shut down like a waterpark in winter!"

#12

What emotional baggage are you carrying that may impact your child's transition to college?

This is an important self-reflection question that helps you recognize any unresolved feelings, fears, or expectations you may have about your child leaving for college. Whether it's your own anxieties about their independence, worries about your relationship with them changing, or even guilt about not being able to do more for them, it's essential to acknowledge these emotions before they influence how you support your teen. By recognizing your own baggage, you can approach the situation with a clear, calm perspective, giving your child the emotional space to navigate their transition without unintentionally carrying the weight of your unresolved feelings. It also allows you to focus on being the supportive presence they need during this exciting yet challenging time. Taking time for self-reflection will help you let go of anything that might hinder your ability to support your child in a healthy, constructive way.

"I went to a college in center city, where muggings, car break-ins, and even assaults were just part of daily life. I didn't realize how much that experience influenced my fears about my daughter going to college."

#13

Children who pay for some or all of their college tuition will often take their education more seriously.

Having skin in the game makes the experience feel more personal and valuable. Whether your child has taken on a part-time job, applied for scholarships, or contributed to tuition, the responsibility of covering even a portion of their education can shift their mindset. They're less likely to take their education for granted, knowing the effort and sacrifice that went into making it possible. This sense of ownership can drive them to attend classes regularly, engage more actively, and put in the hard work necessary to succeed. When they contribute financially, they often realize the actual cost of their education and gain a greater appreciation for the opportunity. As a parent, it's essential to guide them through this process and allow them to feel the weight of their investment. It can be a powerful motivator, helping them take their academic journey more seriously and develop responsibility, time management, and financial planning.

> *"I felt bad that we couldn't afford to pay the entire tuition for my son. He found financial aid and paid about half. The surprising thing is, he took college much more seriously than his friends because he wanted to get his money's worth. Looking back, it was a blessing in disguise."*

#14

Do not take out a parent plus loan.

While it might seem tempting to help ease the financial burden, borrowing in your name can jeopardize your future. Remember, your child is the one attending college, so it's their responsibility to take on student loans. This helps them grasp both the cost and the value of their education. It might also guide them to a school that is both affordable and still gives them the education needed for their desired career. When they borrow money, they must repay it, which encourages them to carefully consider their educational choices, financial planning, and career goals. While you can assist them in exploring scholarships, grants, or work-study opportunities, taking on loans in your name could jeopardize your financial security, especially in retirement. Instead, focus on teaching your child how to manage student loans, understand interest rates, and navigate repayment plans, empowering them to make well-informed decisions.

"I thought I was doing the right thing taking out a parent plus loan, until retirement was on the horizon and I was still paying for my kid's college"

#15

Get a grip on your emotions so you don't make your child feel guilty for going off to college.

It's natural to feel a mix of emotions as they prepare to leave, but managing those feelings is important so they don't negatively impact your child's experience. They're excited for this new chapter and should feel encouraged and supported, not burdened by your sadness or anxiety. While feeling emotional is okay, try to keep those feelings in check when you're around them. Your child needs to think it's OK to go, grow, and embrace their independence without worrying about how it affects you. Remember, this is their time to spread their wings; your role is to cheer them on and ensure they feel confident in their decisions. If you need to cry or process your emotions, do so privately, but keep your focus on helping them step into this exciting new phase of life with excitement, not guilt.

"I was an emotional roller coaster those few months before my son left for school. Thank goodness for close friends and my therapist!"

#16

Approach this time in your child's life with positive energy.

The transition to college is an exciting milestone, not just for them but for you, too. While it's natural to feel a mix of emotions—pride, anxiety, and even a little sadness—try to focus on the incredible opportunities ahead. This is a time for your child to step into their future, and it reflects how much they've grown and how far they've come. Embrace the changes with optimism and enthusiasm and celebrate the adventure ahead. Your attitude will help set the tone for how they view this significant change. Staying upbeat and positive can ease their nerves and help them feel more confident about the transition. This is a time for them to spread their wings, learn new things, and experience life in a whole new way. By showing your support with positive energy, you're cheering them on and teaching them how to embrace change with a hopeful mindset.

"My daughter was more open and comfortable sharing her excitement and fears when I made it a point to approach our conversations with positive energy."

#17

Buying a house near their college as a rental property can be an investment for your child... and yourself!

If you can afford it, consider buying a house in town and using it as a student rental for your child and a few of their friends. The rental income should cover the mortgage payment and a bit more. It also gives them the comfort of living in a place they can call their own, rather than dealing with the uncertainty of dorm life or off-campus housing while keeping a close eye on the property. This arrangement provides your child with a stable living situation. As a bonus, if the house appreciates, you could sell it later for a profit or continue renting it out as an income stream for your own retirement. It's an investment that can offer financial security for your child's college years and potentially benefit your own future as well. However, it's important to make sure the finances work out and that you set clear boundaries and expectations within the lease agreement about rent, upkeep, and responsibilities. It's a win-win situation if done with a solid plan in place.

> *"We were fortunate enough to buy a small house near my son's school, which he and a few friends rented all four years. Knowing their landlord—me!—seemed to keep them diligent about keeping the place clean and relatively party-free. After he graduated, we held onto the property for a few more years, and the rental income turned out to be a great boost to our retirement."*

#18

The more details your child handles on their own, the more prepared they will be at school.

College is full of new responsibilities. Giving your child a chance to manage things like scheduling, paperwork, and even small tasks at home before they leave, builds their independence. When they start taking ownership of their day-to-day needs, they develop essential skills to help them thrive on campus. Handling the details teaches them to problem-solve, manage time, and ask for help when needed—all essential in navigating the college experience. For example, you can give them ownership to have the family cars serviced, which might involve making the appointments, coordinating alternate transportation as well as drop-off and pick-up. By gradually giving them more responsibility, you're setting them up for success and helping them build confidence. They'll feel more capable and less overwhelmed when they face more significant challenges at school, because they've already practiced handling the small ones.

"I was working long hours while my son prepared to leave for school. He handled most of the preparation on his own and I was there to double-check. While I felt guilty for not being around more, I realized it made him so much more resourceful once he got on campus."

#19

Work with your child to plan ahead for move-in day to alleviate stress.

Move-in day can be hectic, but with a little planning, you and your child can make it more manageable and less stressful. Start by creating a game plan together ahead of time, assigning specific duties to each person. For example, one person can take photos of the room while it's empty to document any damage or maintenance issues for the housing office. Another can handle a quick wipe-down of surfaces to freshen up the space. If there's furniture to assemble, designate someone to bring a small toolkit and focus on that task. Additionally, if you've ordered items from local stores for pickup, assign a "runner" to retrieve those or grab any last-minute essentials you may have forgotten. Make a checklist before move-in day to ensure nothing is overlooked. Encourage your child to take the lead in organizing their space so they feel a sense of independence. Be patient with the inevitable hiccups and focus on keeping the atmosphere positive.

> *"We had no structure for move-in day with our first child. Our plan was to load the truck, show up and move-in. While we were in absolute chaos, other families worked together with military precision. We learned our lesson and planned ahead when our second child went off to school."*

#20

When planning for your child's departure,
plan for yourself as well.

As you prepare for your child's departure to college, it's just as important to plan for yourself. This time of transition is a big one for both of you and while it's natural to focus on your child's needs, don't forget about your own. Think about how you can fill the space they're leaving behind with activities, hobbies, or new goals that excite you. Whether it's diving into a new project, rekindling an old passion, or simply allowing yourself some much-needed time to relax and reflect, make sure you're investing in your own happiness too. You've spent years focusing on your child's growth and future—now it's time to refocus a bit on your own. This isn't selfish, it's embracing the opportunity to create a new sense of fulfillment. Plan for your own emotional well-being, stay connected with friends and family, and allow yourself to thrive as you adjust to this new chapter. By doing so, you'll not only ease your own transition, but set a powerful example for your child of how to embrace change with optimism and resilience.

"Nothing's worse than coming home from move-in day
to an empty house. I was not prepared for how quiet the
house was and how alone I felt. My advice to others
would be to make plans for those first few weeks, even if
it's just meeting friends for coffee."

#21

Set up an Uber or Lyft account with your credit card to give your child safe, reliable rides for emergencies.

Setting up an Uber account with your credit card for your child can be a game-changer when they need quick transportation, especially in an unfamiliar place. Let them know it's available whenever they're stuck without a ride or just need a safe, reliable way to get around. It's a great safety net, offering peace of mind that they can access transportation anytime. Just set clear guidelines about responsible use—this isn't a free-for-all, but rather an emergency option or occasional convenience. It's a thoughtful way to support their independence while still looking out for their well-being without hovering.

> *"During high school, I used to be the pick-up mom. So, when my daughter went off to college, I set up an Uber account with my credit card on file. I told her it was my way of picking her up while she was at school. She told me every time she called for an Uber, she felt like I was watching over her, and that made me feel good."*

#22

Encourage your child to pack lightly.

It can be tempting to want to bring everything they might need, but packing too much can create unnecessary stress and make the move feel overwhelming. Encourage your child to focus on the essentials—clothes, toiletries, and a few items that will make their new space feel like home, like a favorite blanket or a few photos. College life often involves much moving around, and having less stuff means less to manage and more flexibility. By packing lightly, they'll also be able to easily adjust to their dorm or apartment, keep their living space organized, and avoid feeling bogged down by clutter. It's a valuable lesson in minimalism and prioritizing what truly matters.

"The lack of storage in a dorm room didn't hit us until move-in day when my daughter realized she packed way too much! We ended up bringing half of her clothes home with us."

#23

Ask your child how they feel about leaving home.

This question allows your child to express their emotions about this big transition. Leaving for college is a mix of excitement and potential sadness, and they may feel both eager for independence and unsure about what's to come. Whether they're excited about the adventure ahead or a little anxious about being away from family, asking this question lets them know you're there to listen and support them through the emotional ups and downs. It also opens a conversation where you can reassure them that feeling a little nervous is completely normal and part of the process. By acknowledging their feelings, you help validate their emotions and create an environment where they feel comfortable sharing what's on their mind. This can help ease the transition, knowing they have your understanding and support as they take this next big step.

"I assumed my son would be happy to leave home and not look back. One day I was helping him pack and he said he was going to miss the smell of my hazelnut coffee in the morning and snuggling on the couch with our dog. The first care package I sent included hazelnut coffee pods and a picture of Max."

#24

Having a joint bank account can be helpful, but don't use it as an excuse to snoop.

While having joint access to a bank account can be helpful for emergencies, don't let it become a way to micromanage your child's financial life. Snooping through every transaction undermines their confidence and sends the message that you don't trust them. Instead, set expectations upfront—explain that the account is there for convenience and as a safety net, not as a tool for control. Use it as an opportunity to teach them about budgeting and financial responsibility but then step back and let them take the reins. If you notice concerning patterns, address them respectfully and constructively, focusing on guidance rather than judgment. Your child is stepping into a world where managing money is a crucial life skill, and they need the freedom to make mistakes and learn from them. Trust is the foundation here—when they feel you're on their side, not over their shoulder, they're more likely to come to you when they need advice.

> *"I had access to my daughter's bank account ever since she opened it for her first part time job. I never thought twice about it until she called from school saying she had nearly one hundred dollars in overdraft fees. Having access to her account let me help her figure out what went sideways and get back on track."*

#25

Save the crying for when your child is not around.

As hard as it may be, try to hold back the deluge of tears when your child is present. Starting college is a huge step for both of you, and while it's perfectly natural to feel emotional, overwhelming them with your own sadness can unintentionally add to their stress. They're already navigating a major life change, and the last thing they need is to feel guilty or anxious about leaving because they see how much it's affecting you. Instead, express how proud you are of them and how excited you are about the new adventures they'll have. It's important they feel confident and ready for this next chapter without worrying about your emotions. Trust that you'll have plenty of time to process everything in your own way, and when you do, you'll do so knowing this is a moment of growth for both of you.

"My son told me to 'get a grip' when he caught me crying one too many times. That was the wakeup call I needed to pull it together and be a positive role model for change."

#26

Encourage your child to plan ahead for healthy
eating while away at college.

Help your child plan ahead by focusing on practical strategies that fit their busy lifestyle. Suggest a basic meal kit: a reusable water bottle, a set of food storage containers, and a few versatile tools like a microwave-safe bowl, a cutting board, and a small knife. If they have access to a kitchen, suggest pantry staples like rice, pasta, canned beans, and spices that can be combined into quick meals. Suggest choosing protein shakes over high-sugar energy drinks. Teach them how to shop smart—buying frozen vegetables for convenience, sticking to store-brand basics to save money, and looking for sales on healthy options. Show dining hall users how to "hack" the menu by combining items, like adding a boiled egg or nuts from the salad bar to a salad for extra protein. Suggest making a habit of prepping snacks, like portioning trail mix or slicing fruit, to avoid mindless snacking during long study sessions. Discuss setting up a basic meal schedule, even if it's flexible, to avoid skipping meals and resorting to fast food.

"My daughter was lucky to have a dorm with a small kitchen. We researched a few dorm-friendly healthy meal hacks. Smoothies, overnight oats and microwave scrambled eggs ended up her favorites."

#27

Minimize culture shock by giving more freedom to your child before they leave for college.

Start giving your child more freedom before they leave for college to ease the transition and prevent culture shock. Let them take on responsibilities like managing curfews, budgeting, and organizing their schedule while they're still under your guidance. This gradual shift helps them build confidence, problem-solving skills, and resilience to feel better prepared to navigate independence. Encourage them to make decisions and learn from their mistakes, even if it's tempting to step in and fix things. For example, removing curfews during the summer allows them to practice balancing late nights with obligations, preparing them for the freedoms and challenges college will bring. This isn't about letting them run wild—it's about creating a space where they can learn to set boundaries and understand how their choices affect their energy and responsibilities. Talk openly about these changes, emphasizing that you're there as a safety net, but trust their ability to make thoughtful decisions. Celebrate their successes, no matter how small, and reassure them that mistakes are part of growth. By giving them the freedom to lead their own life and the tools to handle it wisely, you'll help them transition to college with confidence.

> *"Removing curfew was the hardest thing we did to prepare for my son's departure. He learned how to handle freedom and it let us ease into letting go."*

#28

Ask your child what concerns them the most.

This question invites your child to be open about any worries or fears about college life. They naturally feel some anxiety about the unknown—making new friends, handling the academic workload, or managing their independence. By asking this, you create a safe space for them to share their concerns, giving you the chance to offer support, reassurance, and even practical advice to help ease their worries. Understanding their concerns enables you to address any challenges together before they become overwhelming. It's also a reminder that it's okay to have doubts and that they don't need to face them alone. You can help them brainstorm solutions or listen and offer words of encouragement. This question fosters open communication and lets your child know that no matter their feelings, you're there to listen and support them through it.

"My son shared his number one fear about going off to college was that the dog would die while he was away. That was a complete shocker. Since no one can predict a trip over the rainbow bridge, I made it a point to send pictures often and even had Taz, the dog, Facetime my son (with my help, of course) so he felt connected."

#29

Don't take emotional outbursts personally.

When your child leaves for college, emotions can run high, and they might express feelings in ways that seem out of character—frustration, sadness, or even anger. It's easy to take these outbursts personally but remember that this is a big transition for them. The mixture of excitement, homesickness, and stress can be overwhelming, and your child may be processing it all through emotional reactions. Instead of taking it as a reflection of your relationship, try to approach it with understanding and patience. Your child is feeling a sense of loss and uncertainty, and sometimes, emotions come out as frustration. Give them space to vent and listen without judgment, knowing that these outbursts are part of the adjustment process. Keep calm, offer reassurance, and be a source of comfort. Over time, they'll adapt to the new normal, and these emotional waves will settle. By not taking things personally, you create an open, supportive environment where your child can feel safe expressing their feelings without fearing upsetting you.

"Just when I thought the teenage emotional outbursts couldn't get any worse, the month before my daughter left for college was pretty intense. One minute she was on top of the world, the next, she was a puddle of tears. All I can say is patience became my best friend."

#30

Make sure your child knows how to do laundry.

It's surprising how many students arrive at college without the basic skill of doing laundry. Don't let your child be among them! Laundry might seem trivial, but it's a cornerstone of independence, and mastering it now will save them from stress, and potential embarrassment, later. Take time to teach them the basics, like sorting colors, using the right detergent, reading care labels, and choosing the correct cycle. Have them handle their own laundry the summer before they leave so they feel confident handling it on their own at school. Share tips for communal laundry rooms, like not leaving clothes unattended, and create a simple cheat sheet for reference. This isn't just about clean clothes; it's about building independence and responsibility. A little preparation will save them from stress, and pink socks!

"I learned from my mother putting a bit of distilled vinegar in the wash cycle is a great way to eliminate musty smells from bath towels. Since my son doesn't hang his towels to dry at home, I was pretty sure he wouldn't at school. This turned out to be a simple hack that helped keep his towels fresh."

#31

This is one of the most exciting moments in your child's life.

Sending your child off to college is filled with new opportunities, challenges, and experiences that will shape them into who they are becoming. As parents, it's natural to feel a mix of emotions, but it's important to focus on how incredible this moment is for them. College opens doors to lifelong friendships, new passions, and the chance to discover who they truly are. It's an adventure they'll remember with fondness, even as it stretches them to grow in ways they never imagined. This time is full of promise, and while it may feel like a bittersweet goodbye, it's really a "hello" to the next chapter in their life—a chapter where they get to take the lead and define their path. Embrace this exciting moment, celebrate their achievements, and cheer them on as they step into the world with confidence and excitement. Your support and encouragement will mean the world to them, even if they don't show it.

"I spent so much time worrying about what could go wrong that I forgot to celebrate what was going right. Don't let fear steal the joy of this moment."

Chapter 2
Hugs, Tears and Cheers:
Making Drop-Off a Celebration, Not a Sorrow

#32

Your child will feed off your emotions, so keep them upbeat and positive.

This is a huge moment in their life, and they'll be looking to you for cues on how to feel about it. If you're nervous, overwhelmed, or overly emotional, your child may start to feel anxious or uncertain. Instead, focus on being a steady, uplifting presence. Smile, laugh, and show excitement for the adventures that await them—it will help them feel ready to confidently take on this new chapter. Even if you're secretly holding back tears, project calmness and positivity, reinforcing that you believe in their ability to succeed. Your energy will reassure them and help them approach this transition with a strong, optimistic mindset. Remember, your support and confidence will leave a lasting impression as they take their first steps into independence.

"My daughter told me she didn't feel right being happy when I was so sad. I'm glad she spoke up. It gave us a chance to have a heart-to-heart conversation."

#33

On move-in day, you are there to help, not take control.

This is your child's moment to step into their new life, and while it's natural to want everything to go perfectly, remember that this is about them settling in and finding their own rhythm. Offer support and help with the heavy lifting, then ask your child if they would like your help unpacking or making the bed. Definitely resist the urge to arrange their room, pick their closet setup, or dictate how things should be done. Let them take the lead, even if it means standing back while they figure things out. This day sets the tone for their independence, and by letting them handle the details, you're showing trust in their ability to manage their new space. Focus on being a calming, encouraging presence, rather than adding stress by taking control. However, if they seem to be frozen with indecision, it's okay to take a break and suggest the next steps. This could be exactly what's needed to help them get back on track. Don't linger too long—say your goodbyes, offer a hug, and leave with the confidence that they've got this. Move-in day is a steppingstone for your child, and your support, not your direction, is what will make it a positive start to their new chapter.

"We came to blows over where the desk should go. I was thinking of practicality; my daughter wanted the room to look pretty. Looking back, it wasn't worth the argument."

#34

Let your child think and make decisions for themselves.

Let your child think and make decisions for themselves—it's one of the greatest gifts you can give them as they step into adulthood. While offering advice or jumping in with your own solutions is tempting, stepping back allows them to build confidence in their own judgment. Let them take the lead, whether it's which bed to choose in the dorm, how to set up their desk or closet, or when to introduce themselves to the RA. Be there to guide and support but resist the urge to take over or second-guess their choices. Mistakes are a natural part of learning, and by giving them the space to figure things out, you're helping them grow into independent, capable adults. Trust that they've absorbed the values and lessons you've taught them and are ready to apply them. When you empower them to think critically and make decisions, you're showing them that you believe in their ability to succeed, and that belief is priceless.

> *"My son didn't want to dampen my enthusiasm during move-in, so he let me take care of everything, down to which drawer to use for underwear. Once we left, he changed everything around. I wish I would have let him organize his dorm himself."*

#35

When you feel the urge to take control, step back—
literally—so your child has space to step up.

When you feel the urge to take control, gently excuse yourself—whether it's to get a glass of water, take a brief walk, or pause the conversation—without giving the impression that you're frustrated, dismissive, or throwing your hands up in defeat. You could even excuse yourself to "find" something you left in the car. This small act allows your child to process, reflect, and consider their own solutions without feeling judged or pressured. It also gives you a moment to reset, ensuring your response supports their independence rather than unintentionally undermining it. By stepping back thoughtfully, you're not abandoning them; you're signaling, "I trust you to work through this." That subtle, shift helps your child build confidence, knowing you believe in their ability to handle life's complexities—even when it's hard.

"Being a self-proclaimed control freak, I excused myself
to the bathroom so many times during move-in my
husband asked if I had food poisoning. I told him it was
my way of stepping aside to let my son take the lead."

#36

Hide a little something in their belongings as a surprise.

Slip a little surprise into their belongings—it's a simple but meaningful way to remind your child that you're thinking of them. Whether it's a handwritten note tucked into their suitcase, a favorite treat hidden in their drawer, or a small keepsake that holds sentimental value, it's a sweet gesture that can bring comfort when they need it most. These little surprises can offer a sense of home and warmth during moments of homesickness or stress, and they'll love the thoughtfulness behind it. It's a quiet way to show that even though they're starting a new chapter, you're always there, supporting them from afar.

"My only advice is, don't hide notes too well. My son never found several things I hid for him."

#37

*Move-in day should be an exciting time;
don't make it dramatic.*

Move-in day should be an exciting milestone, not a scene out of a soap opera. Your child is stepping into a new chapter filled with possibilities, and your energy can set the tone for the day. Keep things upbeat and focused on the positive. Avoid turning the day into an overly teary farewell or loading it with dramatic goodbyes. Save the long speeches and emotional moments for a private letter or conversation before the big day. If you need to give some parting wisdom, do so with a short note, hidden for them to find later. This could be the perfect loving gesture of support. Let them feel your pride and support, not your sadness or worry. Let them dive into this new experience with confidence and enthusiasm. A calm, happy goodbye is the best way to show them you believe in their ability to thrive independently. After all, move-in day is about beginnings, not endings—celebrate and cheer them on!

> *"You see it all on move-in day. Some families are super organized, others are a hot mess, yelling and getting angry at each other. Us? We are a pretty chill family, so we moved in and got out of the way."*

#38

Don't make introductions on behalf of your child.

This is your child's time to step forward and start building their own connections. Let them take the lead in saying hello and starting conversations, whether it's meeting roommates, professors, or orientation leaders. While it's natural to want to smooth the way, stepping in sends the message that they need you to navigate social situations, which can undermine their confidence. Instead, encourage them with a smile or a nudge if they seem hesitant, but give them the space to handle it on their own. These small interactions are the building blocks of independence, and learning to introduce themselves and make connections will serve them well throughout life. Your role is to support from the sidelines, not to take the spotlight. Trust that they've got this—they'll appreciate your belief in their abilities and grow stronger because of it.

"My biggest mistake during move-in was introducing myself and my son to everyone... literally, everyone. I was excited; he was mortified. I wanted move-in day to be special, but it ended up stressful, and my son couldn't wait for me to leave."

#39

Keep the focus on your child.

It's their big day, their fresh start, and their journey. It's natural to feel various emotions as you help them transition to college, but remember, this moment isn't about your sadness, worries, or nostalgia. It's about celebrating their growth and supporting their excitement for what lies ahead. Ask how they're feeling, listen to their thoughts, and let them take the lead. Whether it's setting up their room or saying goodbye, your role is to cheer them on and help them feel confident, not to center the day on your feelings or need for control. Be present, patient, and positive, showing them that you're their biggest fan. Keeping the focus on your child reinforces that you're proud of their independence and trust their ability to succeed in this new chapter.

*"The biggest mistake I saw during move-in was when
parents relived their college days the whole time
they were moving their kid into their dorm.
The experience was more about them,
than their child."*

#40

Don't stick around and unpack for your child.

As much as you may want to help them organize their new space or ensure everything is "just right," this is their chance to take ownership of their surroundings and start making their dorm feel like home. Unpacking and arranging their room is part of settling in and becoming comfortable with their independence. Be there to lend a hand with the heavy lifting or offer advice if they ask but resist the urge to take over. Step back, trust their instincts, and give them the space to create a setup that works for them—even if it's not how you would do it. When you let them handle it, you're sending the message that you trust their ability to manage their own life. After all, this is their journey, and figuring out the trivial things is a big step toward building confidence and self-reliance.

"Seriously, your child is going to rearrange everything after you leave anyway. So, be there to unload, do any grunt work, then leave the rest to them."

#41

Make the goodbye short, sweet, and upbeat.

Saying goodbye when dropping your child off at college can be emotional, but keeping it short, sweet, and positive sets the right tone for both of you. It's okay to shed a tear or two—let them know they are tears of happiness and pride—but try not to fall apart. A calm, loving farewell reassures them that you're confident in their ability to thrive and excited for the journey they're about to begin. A hug, a smile, and a few encouraging words are all it takes to show your pride and belief in them. Avoid long, tearful goodbyes that could leave them feeling overwhelmed or guilty; instead, focus on the excitement of this new chapter. Let your child know how much you'll miss them but emphasize that this is their time to spread their wings and grow. By leaving on an upbeat note, you're showing your support and giving them the confidence to embrace the opportunities ahead. Trust that they're ready for this next step and leave them excited about what's ahead, not sad about what's left behind.

"I had a movie-perfect drop-off in mind. I wanted a tender moment, sharing wisdom and final advice, then a long hug and a few tears. In reality, we ended up with campus police urging us to move the car while my daughter was already off making new friends. The goodbye was rushed, and, if I'm being honest, I felt cheated. Looking back, I wish I had shared that wisdom earlier so we could have had a calm, happy goodbye."

#42

As hard as it will be, don't call or text them every day.

While it's natural to want to check in, allowing them the space to adjust to college life without constant reminders of home will help them grow in independence. Allow them to reach out when needed and focus on staying supportive from a distance. If you set up a mutually agreed upon schedule for calls, trust that they'll reach out at that time or when they want to share something. Respect their need to carve out their own path. This balance of giving them space while being there when needed will strengthen their confidence and your relationship.

"That first month was so difficult. Every time I picked up my phone, I wanted to text my daughter, but we had agreed she would text me during the week and we would have a Facetime call on Sundays. I ended up changing my screensaver to a note that said: "It's OK, you'll see her Sunday."

Chapter 3

A Very Special Chapter: Children with Unique Needs

The wisdom in this chapter is meant to provide encouragement while acknowledging that no two situations are the same. As you read, adapt what resonates to fit both you and your child's needs and circumstances. Above all, this chapter is a reminder that you and your child can navigate this new chapter together with patience, flexibility, trust, and support.

#43

Try not to be over-protective.

It's natural to want to shield your child from mistakes or challenges, but remember, they need to experience life on their own to grow and become independent. Over-protectiveness can send the message that you don't trust their ability to handle things, and that can undermine their confidence. Instead, offer support, guidance, and a listening ear when needed, but allow them to face the ups and downs of college life. Trust that you've equipped them with the skills and values to navigate challenges and give them the space to figure things out on their own. While it's hard to let go, stepping back shows your confidence in their ability to succeed and encourages them to develop resilience and problem-solving skills.

#44

Help your child make a strong connection with the Disability Services Office before school starts.

Helping your child with learning differences by establishing a strong connection with the Disability Services Office before school starts is crucial in ensuring they have the support they need to succeed. Start by researching the office's services and learning about the accommodations they provide, such as extended test time, note-taking assistance, or accessible technology. Encourage your child to reach out to the office before the semester begins to register and discuss their specific needs. If possible, set up an introductory meeting with the staff in person or virtually to help your child feel more comfortable and establish a rapport. Empower your child to take the lead during these conversations, as this builds their confidence in advocating for themselves. The staff can provide valuable guidance on navigating academic challenges and connecting with additional resources, such as tutoring or counseling services. Make sure your child understands the process for requesting accommodations and knows how to communicate effectively with professors about their needs. Emphasize that the Disability Services Office is a partner in their success, not a sign of weakness. By forming this connection early, your child will enter college feeling supported and prepared, knowing they have a reliable team to turn to whenever they face challenges.

"I made it a point to visit the Office of Student Accessibility Services (SAS) for every college we toured."

#45

During Admitted Student Day, help your child familiarize him/herself with campus resources.

It's likely you and your child have engaged with the Disability Services Office, perhaps virtually, prior to applying to the college. Admitted Student Day is a great time to visit in person. Encourage your child to ask questions and introduce themselves to staff members—they'll be key allies throughout their college journey. Explore academic support centers where tutoring, study groups, or writing assistance is offered, and make sure your child knows how to access these services. Walk through the campus to locate important spots like the library, counseling center, and quiet spaces where they can recharge when needed. During the day, talk about how they can integrate these resources into their daily routine while maintaining independence. If possible, let them take the lead, asking questions or navigating the campus, as this builds their confidence. Reinforce that these tools and services are there to empower them, not to highlight their differences. By making these connections early, you're setting the foundation for a smoother transition and showing them that support is available whenever they need it.

"Having a child with learning differences can make the college experience even more overwhelming. If you can, start planning earlier than they suggest!"

#46

Plan in advance for medical or therapeutic support.

Planning in advance for medical or therapeutic support is a critical step in setting your child with learning differences up for success in college. Before drop-off, ensure that their medical and therapeutic needs are seamlessly transitioned to their new environment. If they take medications, coordinate with their doctor to arrange prescriptions at a local pharmacy or through a reliable delivery service. For ongoing therapy or specialized care, research local providers near campus and schedule appointments in advance to ensure continuity. Many colleges also offer on-campus counseling or health services, so help your child understand how to access these resources if needed. If applicable, make sure they're registered with the Disability Services Office, which can coordinate accommodation or connect them with further support. Create a clear plan for handling emergencies, like knowing where the nearest urgent care or hospital is located and save these contacts in their phone. Most importantly, involve your child in this process to help them take ownership of their health and well-being. Discuss how to recognize when they need help and encourage them to reach out proactively. By preparing in advance, you'll empower your child to manage their health with confidence while ensuring they have the support network they need to thrive.

"Colleges have, or can help coordinate, just about anything you need to support your child. You just have to ask the right people."

#47

Encourage or help your child create a routine that includes classes, meals, downtime, and self-care.

Creating a routine is essential for helping your child with learning differences thrive in college. Encourage or assist them in designing a schedule that balances classes, meals, downtime, and self-care. Start by working together to map out their class times and ensure they include blocks for meals and snacks to maintain energy and focus throughout the day. Next, help them identify pockets of time for studying and assignments, ensuring it's realistic and avoids last-minute cramming, which can heighten stress. Equally important is carving out downtime—whether it's for relaxing, socializing, or engaging in hobbies that help them recharge. Discuss how self-care practices, like exercise, meditation, or a regular sleep schedule, can support their overall well-being and academic success. Encourage them to write reminders into their phone or planner to stay organized and on track. If they have therapy or other medical appointments, integrate those into the schedule as well, treating them as non-negotiable commitments. While routines can provide structure, flexibility is also important— help them understand how to adjust their schedule as needed without feeling overwhelmed.

"My son's routine was the same as at home, except he set up reminders on his phone since mom wasn't there."

#48

Discuss emergency plans in advance of drop-off.

Before dropping your child off at college, discussing emergency plans is essential to ensure they feel prepared and supported. Start by reviewing key contacts, such as campus security, the nearest urgent care or hospital, and any on-campus counseling or health services. Make sure they have these numbers saved in their phone, along with yours and any other trusted contacts. If your child has specific medical needs, ensure they know how to access their medications, refill prescriptions, or contact a local doctor. Discuss scenarios they might face, like losing their wallet, getting locked out of their dorm, or needing a safe way to get home late at night. Role-play these situations to help them feel confident navigating them on their own. It's also a good idea to set expectations for how you'll communicate in an emergency—whether they call or text first, and how you'll respond to provide calm and steady support. Emphasize that while you trust them to handle challenges, you're always there as a safety net when they truly need help.

"We added a few more ICE (In Case of Emergency)
numbers to my daughter's phone to be sure there were
plenty of options should one of us not be available."

#49

It can be hard to see your child on their own if you've been super-involved during high school.

If you've been super-involved with your child during high school, it can feel especially difficult to step back as they transition to college. You've likely spent years helping them manage schedules, advocating for their needs, and ensuring they stay on track. Now, as they step into independence, it's natural to feel pride, worry, and even loss. However, this is a vital opportunity for both of you to grow. Your child needs the space to take ownership of their choices, navigate challenges, and learn from their mistakes. While stepping back can be uncomfortable, it's essential for building their confidence and resilience. Trust the foundation you've laid and recognize that your role has shifted—you're no longer their manager but their coach and cheerleader. Stay available for guidance, but let them lead the way, whether it's arranging accommodations, managing deadlines, or seeking help when needed. If you find yourself struggling, focus on your own adjustment process. Use this time to rediscover personal interests or hobbies that you may have sidelined. Remember, supporting their independence doesn't mean abandoning them—it means equipping them to thrive on their own terms while knowing you're always in their corner.

"I wish we had eased everyone into independence sooner, including us parents!"

#50

Ensure your child knows the importance of sticking to their medication schedule without changes unless advised by a doctor.

For a child who takes medication, maintaining a consistent schedule is crucial, especially during the transition to college life. With new routines and responsibilities, it's easy for them to forget doses or feel tempted to adjust their medication on their own, but doing so can have serious consequences for their health and well-being. Sit down with your child before they leave for school to discuss the importance of adhering to their prescribed schedule and what to do if they accidentally miss a dose. Ensure they understand that any changes to their medication should always be made under the guidance of their doctor. Encourage them to set reminders on their phone or use a pill organizer to help them stay on track. If they're nervous about managing this responsibility, consider scheduling a virtual or in-person check-in with their doctor to reinforce these points and build their confidence. Additionally, make sure they know how to refill their prescriptions, where to find a local pharmacy near campus, and how to handle emergencies, such as losing their medication.

"Since my son really likes his doctor, I had her stress the importance to my son for keeping up with prescriptions."

#51

Stay alert to sudden changes in your child's behavior and create a safe space for honest conversations.

For students with special needs, sudden changes in behavior can sometimes signal more than the usual college stress—they may indicate deeper struggles related to mental health, sensory overload, medication adjustments, or social challenges. Because your child may already be managing complex emotional or developmental needs, it's crucial to stay attuned to shifts in mood, routines, or communication patterns. If you notice concerning changes, reach out with compassion and clarity. Ask direct but gentle questions like, "Are you feeling overwhelmed?" or "Do you feel safe and supported?" Your child might not always have the words to express what's wrong, so your calm, nonjudgmental approach can make it easier for them to open up. If they do, listen without rushing to fix it—sometimes, feeling heard is the first step toward healing. Partner with campus disability services, mental health resources, or medical professionals as needed. Your steady, supportive presence can be their anchor in uncertain moments.

"When my daughter started acting out of character, we didn't grill her for details. Rather, we asked if we could come visit, saying we really missed her. We quickly saw there was friction between her and her roommate."

#52

Ask your child: "If you begin to have challenges at school, how would you like me to support you?"

Having an open conversation with your child about how they'd like you to support them if they face challenges at school is an essential step in fostering independence and trust. Asking them, "If you begin to have challenges at school, how would you like me to support you?" shows that you respect their autonomy and value their input. It invites them to reflect on what kind of help feels meaningful and empowering to them, whether it's simply listening, offering advice, or helping them identify resources. This approach helps avoid the frustration or overwhelm that can come when parents jump in uninvited to fix problems. By asking for their "permission" to help, you're reinforcing the idea that they're in charge of navigating their college journey while also reminding them that they don't have to face struggles alone. Encourage them to think about specific ways you can provide support, such as being a sounding board or helping them connect with campus resources like advisors or tutors. This dialogue also sets the tone for ongoing, open communication where they feel comfortable reaching out when needed. By respecting their preferences and boundaries, you're building a strong, collaborative relationship, and equipping them to face challenges with confidence.

"After overstepping one too many times, I finally asked my son how he wanted us to help. All he really needed was for us to be a sounding board."

#53

Find and join a support group that fits you and your child's situation.

A support group that aligns with you and your child's situation can be an invaluable source of support and information. These groups often cater to specific needs, such as parents of college students with learning differences, disability advocacy, or navigating college life in general. Being part of a community of parents who've been through similar experiences allows you to ask questions, share advice, and gain insights into challenges and solutions you might not have considered. These groups can be especially helpful when you feel uncertain or overwhelmed—there's comfort in knowing others understand what you're going through. Look for groups that encourage positivity, collaboration, and shared learning. Avoid groups that focus solely on complaints or negativity. Many groups also share resources, such as tips for accessing campus accommodations, recommendations for assistive technology, or advice for navigating difficult conversations with professors or administrators. Encourage your child to join a relevant group for students, if appropriate, so they can connect with peers facing similar challenges. Engaging with these communities provides practical advice and helps you feel less alone in the journey.

"It took me a few tries before finding the right parents' group. Some were too judgmental."

#54

Both you and your child should keep copies of all documents required by the Disability Services Office.

Documents, such as medical evaluations, Individualized Education Plans (IEPs), 504 plans, or accommodation letters—serve as the foundation for accessing support and ensuring your child's needs are met. Make sure you both have copies stored in an organized, accessible way, such as in a physical folder and on a cloud-based platform like Google Drive. This ensures the information is easily retrievable if your child needs to re-submit documentation or reference it later. It's also helpful if the Disability Services Office requests updates or additional paperwork during the semester. Encourage your child to take ownership of these documents, as it reinforces their responsibility and self-advocacy skills. While it's crucial to let them manage their accommodations independently, having a backup copy yourself offers peace of mind in case anything is lost or forgotten. Review these documents together to ensure your child understands their rights and how to utilize their accommodations effectively. Keeping everything organized and accessible empowers your child to confidently navigate college, while you remain a reliable resource in supporting their success.

"My daughter was a bit disorganized when it came to paperwork, so we helped get everything in order, then suggested she keep the file in her in-room safe and we had a copy of everything as a handy backup."

Chapter 4

Your Job Isn't Over, It's Evolved:
How to Support Their Growth Without
Taking the Spotlight

#55

Guide your child to be their own superhero.

Don't try to be a superhero who saves your child. When your student calls home thinking the world is on fire and everyone is the bad guy, your first instinct might be to swoop in and solve everything. But resist that urge. Instead, listen carefully to what they're saying, ask thoughtful questions to help them process their emotions, and offer reassurance that they can handle whatever challenges come their way. Let them know you're there for support but encourage them to find their own solutions. This is a key part of their growth and independence—they need to learn how to navigate problems on their own, even if they seem overwhelming now. By stepping back and letting them be the hero of their own story, you're giving them the confidence to tackle life's challenges, knowing that they can overcome them. They may not have all the answers yet, but they'll figure it out—and you'll be there to cheer them on every step of the way.

> *"Best part of freshman year was my daughter calling to announce she fixed the sink all by herself!"*

#56

---

*Send care packages, especially
during finals week!*

Sending a care package filled with snacks, familiar comforts, and a few personal touches is a powerful way to remind your child of home while they embrace their independence. It's a small gesture with a big impact, creating a bridge between their new life and the one they've always known. Including their favorite treats, cherished photos, or a snapshot of a special memory. brings comfort and reassurance, especially during moments of homesickness or stress. Care packages are especially meaningful during finals week, when stress levels peak and a little encouragement goes a long way. Fill the package with study snacks, stress-relief items, or even a handwritten note expressing your pride and support. These thoughtful surprises show them you're thinking of them. They can also offer a boost of energy and emotional comfort when they need it most. Sending care packages regularly, once a month, for example, keeps your connection strong, reminding them that while they're growing and thriving independently, they're still deeply rooted in the love and support of home. It's a simple way to stay close and let them know they're never far from your thoughts, even miles away.

> *"If you're sending a care package for finals week, make sure it arrives a week or so before the actual tests. My first care package arrived a day <u>after</u> she took her tests; so, it ended up being a 'congratulations on finishing' package."*

#57

Be intentional about keeping lines of communication open.

Be intentional about keeping the lines of communication open with your child, but remember, no judgment. The goal is to create a space where they feel comfortable sharing anything—whether it's excitement, struggles, or even mistakes—without fear of harsh criticism. Regular check-ins through texts, calls, or video chats can help maintain a strong connection, but it's essential that they know you're there to listen, not judge. If they feel they can't be open with you about their experiences, they'll be less likely to reach out when they need support. When you approach conversations with empathy, understanding, and no immediate problem-solving or criticism, you create a safe space for them to grow.

> *"I didn't want to seem like a nosy parent, so I would only ask 'yes' and 'no' questions. It wasn't until I started asking more open-ended questions that our conversations became more meaningful."*

#58

The first few months will be nerve-wracking. Lean on other parents... NOT your child.

Feeling anxious as your child adjusts to their new life is natural, but leaning on them for reassurance can create unnecessary pressure. Instead, seek support from parents who have already navigated this journey. Those who have survived the first few years of college can offer valuable insights, advice, and encouragement. Their experience can ease your nerves, provide a fresh perspective, and remind you that this transition is manageable. While connecting with parents of brand-new college students might seem helpful, it can sometimes amplify shared anxieties. Turning to seasoned parents helps you build a positive, informed support network, allowing you to process your emotions while staying focused on being your child's cheerleader as they embark on this exciting chapter.

> *"My daughter would always ask me, "How are you doing?" She really didn't need to hear that I was a wreck. I would tell her I missed her, but I'm excited for her at the same time. Then, I'd call a girlfriend and let it out just how sad I really was. Over time, it got better, but those first few months were quite the adjustment."*

#59

Changing from parent/child to adult/adult relationship can be difficult; recognize when you need help.

The transition from a parent/child relationship to an adult/adult dynamic can be one of the most challenging aspects of your child going to college. Suddenly, the routines and roles you've relied on for years shift, leaving you to navigate uncharted emotional territory. It's normal to feel pride, loss, and uncertainty as you adjust to this new phase of your relationship. However, if you find yourself struggling feeling overwhelmed, anxious, or stuck, it's important to recognize when you might need additional support. Talking with a counselor or joining a support group for parents can help you process these emotions and develop strategies for fostering a healthy relationship with your child. A therapist can offer perspective and tools to help you maintain the balance of giving them space to grow, while also maintaining a meaningful connection. Seeking help isn't a sign of failure—it's a way to care for yourself and ensure you're equipped to handle the challenges of this transition. Remember, your well-being is just as important as your child's, and addressing your feelings can strengthen both your sense of self and your evolving relationship.

"We had an adult sit-down when my daughter came home for winter break. We were honest with her that the transition from parent to supporter was more challenging than we expected, and we needed her patience while we got comfortable with our new role."

#60

Resist the urge to jump in and fix everything for your child.

When the urge to step in and fix things arises, pause and reflect on your experiences. Think about a time when you faced challenges or made mistakes in your own life. Did you want your parents to swoop in and take over, or did you prefer to handle things yourself, even if it meant struggling a little? Remember that your child, just like you once did, needs the space to figure things out independently. They might not always get it right, but learning from their mistakes is part of growing up. By stepping back, you show them that you trust their ability to navigate challenges, and that trust is far more empowering than any solution you could offer. Remember, you are there to support them in becoming resourceful, successful, and happy adults.

"Every time I had the urge to jump in and fix something for my son, I thought back to my overly involved parents and how mortified I was when they just showed up every weekend to 'help.' I was committed to not repeat the pattern."

#61

"What do you think you should do?" is the most powerful response to help your child become more independent.

When your child calls with a problem, it's tempting to jump in with solutions. After all, you've spent years guiding them through life's challenges. But in college, the goal shifts from solving their problems to helping them build the confidence to solve their own. Asking, "What do you think you should do?" gently places the responsibility back in their hands. It signals that you trust their judgment and believe they're capable of making sound decisions. This question encourages critical thinking, problem-solving, and self-reflection—skills they'll need far beyond the classroom. Even if they stumble, the process of considering their options and making a choice fosters growth. It also shifts your role from fixer to supporter, a necessary transition as they navigate adulthood. The next time they call in a panic, resist the urge to fix it. Instead, ask that simple, powerful question—and watch them rise to the occasion.

"A friend gave me some tough love, reminding me that each time I took over, I was stealing independence from my son. She suggested I respond with, 'That's interesting; what do you think you should do?' After the first few times, my son began hunting down resources at school to help him. The difference in his level of independence from the beginning to the end of his first year was amazing!"

#62

Don't assume your child doesn't want to talk to you.

It's easy to think that they're too busy or have outgrown the need for your support, but often, they crave that connection. Hopefully, you've established a mutually agreed-upon schedule to connect, so honor that schedule, and let them know you're there to listen. Even if they don't always pick up the phone right away, still attempt to connect. If they are not available, leave a brief, "I'm thinking about you" message. Sometimes they may just need a reminder that you're available for a chat without pressure, or they're processing things on their own before reaching out. Create a comfortable space for open communication by showing interest in their life but also respecting their need for space. A simple "How's everything going?" can open the door to a deeper conversation. Keep the lines open, even if it feels like they're pulling away. You might be surprised at how much they still want to share, and your willingness to listen without judgment can strengthen your bond, no matter the distance.

"Our son was never a big talker. When he came home for break, I assumed he would let me know if he wanted to talk, so I gave him space and didn't press for details. Years later he told me he actually felt a bit abandoned. Learn from my mistake! Don't assume they don't want to share. Sometimes they just need a bit of prodding."

#63

Become unflappable.

As your child grows into their independence during college, you might notice changes that catch you off guard—a new hair color, a nose ring, or even a tattoo. While it's natural to feel surprised, staying calm and avoiding overreaction is important. These changes are often a form of self-expression and exploration, not a rejection of your values or your relationship. Becoming unflappable in these moments helps maintain a strong connection with your child, showing them that your love and support are unwavering, even as they explore their identity. While a nose ring or hair dye is temporary, a tattoo is permanent—but it doesn't have to have a permanent, negative effect on your relationship. Instead of focusing on the choice itself, consider the bigger picture: your child is growing, learning, and figuring out who they are. If you feel the need to address your feelings, do so in a calm, non-judgmental way, but remember that their choices are their own. By responding with understanding and openness, you create an environment where they feel safe sharing their life with you.

"Our first son came home with a new tattoo. We overreacted and it took a long time for us to rebuild our relationship. With our second child, I got smart and would ask, 'Are there any big changes we should be prepared for?' We learned our lesson and managed our reaction to pink hair much, much better!"

#64

Your child will screw up... they must learn to pay the consequence.

Making mistakes is part of growing up, learning, and gaining independence. The important thing is that they learn from their mistakes and understand the consequences of their actions. While it's hard to watch them face challenges or failures, it's necessary for their growth. Don't rush in to fix things or shield them from every bump in the road. Instead, let them experience the natural outcomes of their choices and offer guidance when asked. This helps them learn to navigate these situations on their own. This will teach them responsibility, accountability, and resilience. You've given them the tools; now it's time for them to apply them. Trust that, even through mistakes, they're gaining valuable life lessons that will serve them in the future.

"My son called in a panic when he didn't get the classes he needed because he waited until the last minute to register. He wanted me to 'do something.' I suggested he speak to his academic advisor. That really ticked him off, but he learned a painful lesson and took a summer class to catch up. Oh, and he never registered late again!"

#65

When your child visits, let them know that laundry stays at school.

When your child comes home for a visit, it's tempting to do their laundry for them, but this is an excellent opportunity to reinforce their independence. Let them know that laundry stays at school. It's a small yet significant way to remind them that they can manage the everyday responsibilities of living independently. Of course, you can offer to help with other things—like stocking their fridge with favorite snacks or lending an ear—but laundry is one of those life skills they need to handle themselves. Encourage them to use their time at home to relax and recharge, not to slip back into the old habits of relying on you for every little thing. This approach teaches them responsibility while also creating a healthy boundary that reinforces their growing independence. Plus, it helps them get into the routine of managing their chores, so when they're back at school, they can feel more confident in taking care of the basics on their own.

"The first time my son came home, I told him, I wanted to see him, not his laundry."

#66

Set expectations in advance for when your child wants to bring home a new boyfriend or girlfriend.

If your child plans to bring a boyfriend or girlfriend home during the holiday break, it's important to have a conversation in advance about expectations, especially regarding sleeping arrangements. This can help avoid any uncomfortable surprises or misunderstandings during their visit. Start by discussing your house rules in a calm and respectful manner, clearly outlining what you're comfortable with, while being open to hearing their perspective. For example, you might say, "We're excited to have your guest stay with us. Let's talk about how we can make everyone feel comfortable while respecting the rules of our home." Approach the conversation as a dialogue, not a lecture, and explain your reasoning if needed, such as wanting to maintain boundaries or traditions that are meaningful to your family. If a compromise is possible, explore options like separate rooms or sleeping areas, and ensure their guest feels welcomed and respected. Framing the conversation as a collaborative effort shows your child that you value their independence, while balancing it with your own comfort level. By addressing this ahead of time, you set clear expectations, reduce tension, and create an environment where everyone can enjoy the holidays together.

"In front of her new boyfriend, I told—ok, yelled—at my daughter 'You're not sleeping him in my house!' She was mortified and didn't come home for the rest of the year. We both agreed to communicate better and compromise going forward."

#67

Learn to listen without judging or adding undue pressure.

When your child shares their thoughts or struggles, listen with an open heart and mind, avoiding the urge to judge or "fix" everything. Often, they simply need a sounding board, validation, or space to process their emotions. By actively listening without interrupting or jumping in with solutions, you show respect for their independence and build trust. Pay attention not only to their words but also to the emotions behind them—they may need reassurance or just the freedom to express themselves without added pressure. Validating their feelings and showing empathy creates a safe, non-judgmental space where they can share openly, knowing their thoughts and emotions matter. This approach fosters a foundation of honest communication, where they feel supported as they navigate their path while you demonstrate your trust in their ability to figure things out. Your quiet presence and willingness to listen deeply will go further in building their confidence and independence than any quick fix ever could. You provide the understanding and encouragement they need to grow by simply being there for them.

"It seemed my go-to response in every conversation was, 'Tell me more.' That simple response gave me time to process what I was hearing. Those three words saved many an argument over her four years away!"

#68

You can stop now if you've been monitoring your child's grades.

You've done your part in preparing them for this moment, and now it's up to them to take responsibility for their academic journey. Trust that they know how to ask for help if needed, and that they're learning to manage their time and responsibilities on their own. Constantly checking in on their grades might create unnecessary pressure or give them the impression that you don't trust them to handle things. Instead, empower your child by giving them the space to manage their own progress. Encourage open communication so they feel comfortable reaching out if they're struggling but avoid hovering or micromanaging. It's a big step for them—and for you—to let go of the need to monitor every little detail. It's time for them to grow into their independence, make mistakes, learn from them, and celebrate successes. You've set the foundation, now trust that they'll use it to navigate their academic path, with the confidence that you're there to support them if they need it.

"We agreed that we would continue to help pay tuition as long as our son shared his grades with us monthly. This gave him ownership for his grades, while we stayed in the loop."

#69

---

*Be aware of sudden changes in your child's behavior
and encourage open conversation.*

Suppose you notice sudden, significant changes in your child's demeanor, especially if they seem off or distant. If their actions or social media posts raise red flags, don't hesitate to reach out and ask tough questions like, "Are you feeling depressed?" or "Are you safe?" It might be uncomfortable, but addressing these concerns head-on is crucial. If they are struggling, be ready to listen without judgment and support them fully. There are resources available— like counseling services on campus or mental health hotlines—that can help. Just don't ignore their answers or brush things off. Even if they brush you off in return, stay persistent. Let them know you're there to support them no matter what and that their well-being is the most important thing. Encouraging them to seek help and offering to guide them toward the right resources can make all the difference. Whether they admit it or not, your child needs to know that you see them, care for them, and are ready to help them through any challenges they face.

*"During those first few months, I chalked up behavior
changes to my son simply adjusting to college. It wasn't
until winter break that we realized he had a serious
problem. Looking back, there were red flags I could
have picked up on but didn't."*

#70

Calm down! It will help your child chill, too.

When you feel your stress levels rising, remember that your calmness will help your child stay grounded, too. Getting caught up in the whirlwind of emotions and worries as they head off to college is easy, but staying calm and composed gives your child the reassurance they need. If you're anxious, they're likely to pick up on it and feel more uncertain or overwhelmed. By managing your stress, you set a positive example of approaching change with confidence and grace. Take a deep breath, focus on the exciting opportunities ahead, and remind yourself that this is a big moment of growth—for both you and your child. It's a learning curve, and it's okay if things feel a little chaotic. Keeping a calm demeanor allows your child to do the same, knowing they have the emotional stability to navigate their new journey. Trust that they'll find their rhythm; your peaceful presence will help them feel ready to tackle the challenges ahead. You've prepared them well, and now it's time to let them take the reins—without adding unnecessary stress to the equation.

> *"I used to start nearly every phone call asking why my daughter didn't call or text more often. That set a stressful tone for our conversation. Then I started simply saying, 'I'm so happy to hear your voice,' and it made all the difference."*

#71

You will spend more time thinking about your child than they spend thinking of you.

It's a hard truth to accept, but during this time of transition, you'll spend more time thinking about your child then they'll spend thinking of you. They're off on their own, meeting new people, tackling new challenges, and discovering who they are away from home. While you may constantly be wondering how they're doing, they're busy navigating their new world and figuring things out for themselves. It's completely natural to feel this way—after all, you've invested so much in getting them to this point. But remember, it's a sign of their growth and independence. This is a part of the process: letting them go so they can find their own path, even if that means they're not texting you every day. Your role now is to support them from a distance and give them the space they need to thrive. Trust that they're thinking of you in their own way, but don't take it personally if they're not as tuned into home life as you are. It's not a reflection of how much they love you; it's a sign they're gaining the confidence to stand on their own two feet. And, before you know it, they'll be back home to reconnect and share their new experiences.

> *"I was crushed the first time my daughter forgot my birthday, but in reality, she was super busy with rushing for a sorority and a heavy courseload. I got over it, but we agreed to celebrate the next time she came home."*

#72

Don't smother your child when they come home for a visit.

When your child returns home for a visit, it's important to be welcoming and respectful of their newfound independence. After being away at college, they've grown and changed, and they might want a little space to adjust back into the family dynamic. Avoid nagging or treating them like they're still living under your roof full-time. Remember, they've been making their own decisions and managing their time and responsibilities. If you smother them with rules, questions, or constant reminders, it can feel suffocating. The last thing you want is for them to feel like they're under a microscope when they come home, which could make them less likely to return for future visits. Be nice, keep it light, and enjoy the time together without pushing too hard. Offer a balance of support and space: ask about their life, listen to their stories, and give them room to breathe. Treating them like the young adult they are helps nurture the relationship, making it more likely that they'll want to come back and reconnect with you again and again. When they feel respected and trusted, they'll be more comfortable being themselves, and the time spent together will be more meaningful for both of you.

"Things were different when my son came home for break. I wanted to spend time with him and hear about everything that was happening at school. All he wanted to do was sleep."

#73

Treat your child like the adult they are growing into.

Recognize that this is their time to step into independence. While you've been guiding and supporting them for years, respecting their ability to make decisions and handle challenges independently is important. This doesn't mean withdrawing support but shifting from the constant advice-giver role to one of encouragement and trust. Let them make their own mistakes and learn from them while offering a listening ear when needed. By showing them respect and treating them as capable adults, you empower them to take ownership of their choices, boost their confidence, and prepare them for life after college. This shift can be tough, but it's crucial for their growth—a sign that you're ready to cheer them on as they spread their wings.

"The biggest lesson for me was to stop questioning my daughter's every choice. Sure, she made some mistakes, but she owned up, learned and moved on. And, in the end, isn't that what we all want for our kids?"

#74

You can't control everything that your child does in college.

This is their time to experiment, make mistakes, and learn to manage responsibilities on their own. While it can be tough to watch them face challenges, it's important to remember that these struggles are a natural part of growing up. What they need most during this time is to know that you're there for them—ready to listen, support, and offer guidance when they need it. Your role isn't to step in and fix everything, but to be a steady presence in their corner, reminding them that they can handle whatever comes their way. Even if they stumble, showing unconditional love and trust will give them the confidence to get back up and keep going. Let them know you're proud of their progress and that you'll always be there when they need a safety net, no matter how far they go.

"My son felt strongly about joining a fraternity. Even though it was really tough that first year and I thought he should quit, he ended up having a really great experience. If he would have listened to me, he would have missed out on a brotherhood that supported him through some pretty rough patches."

#75

Your child might not call often (and it's OK).

Your child might not call as often as you'd like, and that's okay—it's a natural part of their journey toward independence. College is a time of personal growth, and they're learning to balance time, friendships, and responsibilities. While it's natural to miss them, try not to take their silence personally. They may simply be caught up in new experiences or embracing the space to figure things out on their own. If you've set a regular schedule for connecting, approach any missed check-ins with understanding. Let them know you're a little bummed you haven't connected but understand they're busy. Suggest another time to talk without adding pressure. In the meantime, focus on sending supportive messages or light check-ins to remind them you're there. Trust that when they need you, they'll reach out. Respect their need for space while keeping communication open so they always feel supported when they're ready to reconnect.

> *"Some friends had a set time each week to call their child. That didn't work for us. My daughter was in a sorority and always super busy. We agreed to connect somehow—text, call, or email—every week or so, and that would be enough. This took the pressure off and made it really special when we did catch up."*

#76

Let them go but remind them you're still nearby.

Letting go is one of the hardest parts of parenting, especially when your child heads off to college. But as challenging as it is, giving them the freedom to spread their wings and navigate life on their own is essential. That said, it's just as important to remind them that you're still there for them, even if they're miles away. A simple text, phone call, or care package can go a long way in showing your support. Let them know they have the space to grow, but provide reassurance that they're never alone in the process. You don't need to hover or interfere, but a gentle reminder that you're nearby if they need advice or a listening ear can help them feel secure. Letting them take the lead in their journey while being a steady presence from afar helps them find their balance between independence and connection. You'll always be their foundation, waiting for the moment they need to lean on you.

"I sent a card to my son that said something like, 'I'm just a phone call away.' He still has it fifteen years later."

#77

Empower your child to advocate for themselves.

It's tempting to step in and handle things for them, but the best way to grow is by learning to speak up and take charge of their own needs. Whether dealing with professors, seeking help from campus resources, or resolving conflicts with roommates, encourage them to voice their concerns and ask for what they need. Let them know that it's okay to speak up for themselves and that they have the right to stand up for their well-being academically and personally. By doing this, you're helping them develop confidence and problem-solving skills that will serve them well throughout life. While you can offer advice and support, the goal is for them to feel empowered to handle challenges independently. The more they practice advocating for themselves, the more capable and self-assured they'll become.

"We encouraged our daughter to stand up for herself, and she did! Now she works on behalf of underprivileged youth. It's awesome to see her making a difference."

#78

Be available but keep your distance.

Being available for your child while keeping a respectful distance can be a delicate balance. You want to be there for them when they need you, but you also want to give them the space to grow, solve problems, and manage their new independence. Let them know you're just a phone call or message away, but don't rush in whenever they face a challenge. Encourage them to reach out when they need advice or support but also trust that they can handle things independently. This gives your child the confidence to figure things out themself while knowing they have a safety net if needed. It's about being a quiet, steady presence—there for guidance but not overbearing. This approach helps your child feel empowered and more self-reliant while still maintaining the bond that's so important during this transition. Keep the lines of communication open but allow them to take the lead on when and how they reach out. Let them know that you're there to listen, not to solve, and that their independence is something you celebrate, even as you're always ready to support them from a distance.

"Standing back while my son worked through changing his major and readjusting his schedule was hard. I wanted to jump in and help. He made some decisions I didn't understand, but it all worked out in the end, and I had a newfound appreciation for how he approached bumps in the road."

#79

*Expect a roller-coaster of emotions, especially
in the first year.*

Your child will experience highs and lows as they adjust to new independence, and you might feel like you're on that emotional ride with them. But here's the trick—don't get on the rollercoaster yourself. It's tempting to feel every twist and turn, but if you let yourself get caught up in their ups and downs, it can create unnecessary stress for both of you. Instead, stay grounded and be a calm, supportive presence when they need it. Trust that they will figure things out and grow through the process, even if it gets tough at times. Your role is to offer encouragement and let them know you're there for them without getting swept up in the chaos. This gives them the emotional space they need to face challenges head-on, and it helps them maintain balance during this big transition. Just remember—this is all part of the journey, and as long as you stay steady, they will, too.

*"It seemed like we had a different child each time our
daughter came home on break. She was trying so many
different clubs and activities to see what felt right. Once
she found her tribe with the entrepreneur club,
she seemed to settle in, thank goodness!"*

#80

*Prepare in advance for the "I want to change colleges"
or "I want to drop out" conversations.*

The first semester of college is a significant adjustment, and it's common for students to feel overwhelmed and question their decisions. Many students have a knee-jerk reaction and express a desire to drop out or transfer colleges when things feel difficult. As a parent, preparing for these conversations in advance is important so you can respond calmly and constructively. Start by normalizing these feelings before they leave for college, letting them know that it's common to face challenges in the beginning. If the conversation arises, avoid reacting emotionally or dismissing their concerns. Instead, listen to their frustrations with an open mind and encourage them to pinpoint what's causing their distress. Is it academic pressure, homesickness, or difficulty making friends? Once you identify the root of the issue, you can help them explore solutions, such as using campus resources, adjusting their schedule, or giving themselves more time to settle in. Remind them that transitions are rarely easy, but that perseverance often leads to rewarding experiences. Encourage them to wait until the end of the semester or year before making big decisions, as many initial challenges tend to improve over time.

*"At Thanksgiving our son announced he was planning
to switch colleges. After the initial 'What the Heck??!!'
reaction, we talked it through, gave him some advice
and he agreed to stick it out for a full year."*

#81

Encourage independence and initiative.

Letting your child make decisions, handle responsibilities, and solve problems independently can feel uncomfortable, but it's one of the most valuable gifts you can give them. By stepping back, you're encouraging them to take initiative, build confidence, and trust their ability to navigate challenges. When they encounter problems, resist the urge to jump in and fix everything. Instead, guide them toward the right resources—like campus advisors, counselors, or academic support—and encourage them to seek help on their own. This teaches them how to utilize support systems and reinforces their responsibility for managing their own challenges. Your role is to support and guide, not to solve. The more you allow them to take charge, the more they'll develop the independence and resilience needed for adulthood. Letting them lead fosters a sense of accomplishment and shows them they're capable of handling both successes and setbacks. By stepping back, you empower your child to grow and develop essential problem-solving skills, while giving them the reassurance that you're always in their corner when truly needed. It's not easy but allowing them to take the reins is crucial in helping them thrive.

"Once my daughter left for college, I got so busy with new hobbies that I was rarely available at a moment's notice to talk things through. My daughter became super self-sufficient and would call to share her latest triumph. I never felt guilty for being busy."

#82

*Find effective ways to deal with the new boundaries
your child gives you.*

Respect the new boundaries your child sets as they adjust to life in college—it's a natural part of their journey toward independence. While it can be tough when they pull back, it's important to honor their need for space while continuing to offer support from a distance. They're learning to manage their own life, which often involves redefining the relationship and setting new expectations. Trust the foundation you've built together and remind yourself that these boundaries aren't a rejection of your love—they're a sign of their growth. Finding ways to center yourself, whether through mindfulness, meditation, reflection, or simply quiet moments of gratitude, can help you navigate this transition. Focus on their safety, success, and well-being while trusting in their ability to handle the challenges ahead. By giving them space and showing faith in their growth, you're supporting them as they become the person they're meant to be.

*"I won't lie… the transition was tough. I took up yoga,
my husband started helping a friend remodel an old
car, and we started golfing together. We each had our
own way of dealing with the new normal."*

#83

Your child was born with wings... now is the time to fly!

This is the moment you've been preparing for: when your child spreads their wings and takes on the world. It's natural to feel emotional but remember that this is a success for both of you. All those years of love, guidance, and teaching have led to this milestone where they're ready to embrace their independence. Your role has shifted from caregiver to cheerleader, supporting them as they navigate this exciting new chapter. Trust in the foundation you've built together, knowing that the skills and values you've instilled will guide them. It's not about letting go completely, but about stepping back with pride and celebrating their growth. Take a moment to acknowledge the areas that feel hardest to let go, and plan ways to respond positively and supportively. By cheering them on and showing your belief in their abilities, you're sending a powerful message of confidence and love. This is their time to shine, and your encouragement will help them thrive as they create their own path. Let them fly and take pride in the incredible journey you've shared to get to this point.

"A friend pulled me aside one day for some tough love. She pointed out by continually doing so much for my son, I was actually crippling him from becoming an adult. It was hard to hear, but it was needed."

Chapter 5
Parent 2.0: Redefining Your Role and Rediscovering Yourself

#84

*Don't think of yourself as an empty nester...
think of yourself as a bird launcher.*

This shift in perspective changes everything. You're not losing your child to college—you're helping them take flight into their own life. You've spent years nurturing them, giving them the skills and wisdom they need to spread their wings, and now it's time for them to soar. Your role isn't over; it's just transformed. You're still a support system, a guide, and a cheerleader, but now you're watching them chart their own course. It's exciting to think of it this way! Just as a bird takes off into the world, there's a sense of pride and purpose in knowing your child is ready to face new challenges, pursue their dreams, and grow into the person they were meant to be. Let go of the sadness of seeing their empty bedroom and embrace the joy of seeing them launch into their next adventure. Your job is to encourage them from the sidelines, offering love and guidance, and enjoy watching them fly.

*"The transition was easier when I realized you look
<u>backwards</u> to an empty nest; but you look <u>forward</u> to
see the baby bird that just launched."*

#85

---

*Make non-negotiable plans for something
fun the day after drop-off!*

The day after drop-off is the perfect time to focus on yourself and recharge. Make non-negotiable plans for something fun that will give you a chance to unwind and enjoy a break. Whether it's a day trip, a spa visit, or catching up with friends, having something enjoyable on the calendar will help ease the emotional rollercoaster of saying goodbye. If you make this something you've purchased tickets for, bailing on the event will be that much harder. It's a chance to refuel, so you can return home with a fresh perspective and be ready to embrace this new chapter with positivity. Taking care of yourself isn't selfish—it's necessary.

> *"The best advice I got was to book something fun for the day or week after drop-off and commit to not cancelling. It game me something not child-related to look forward to."*

#86

---

*Be gentle with yourself and acknowledge the
big changes in your life.*

As your child heads off to college, being gentle with yourself is essential. This transition marks a significant change, and it's natural to feel a mix of pride, sadness, excitement, and even uncertainty. Give yourself permission to feel it all without judgment. Acknowledge that this is a big step, not just for your child but for you as well. Your role is shifting, and it's okay to take time to adjust. There's no timeline for processing these emotions; you don't need to rush through them. It's important to show yourself compassion and understand that this transition is an opportunity for both you and your child to grow. Allow yourself to reflect on the years spent nurturing and guiding and celebrate the progress you've both made. Change is hard, but it also brings new possibilities. Be kind to yourself through this journey, and trust that it will get easier with time.

> *"I think most of my problems adjusting came from beating myself up about what I could have or should have done differently during my son's senior year in high school. I should have made him study more; I should have made him save more money, I should have blah, blah blah. Sometimes you just have to give yourself some grace and realize the past is the past, you just have to let it go."*

#87

Have a response prepared for when someone asks why you are not devastated and sad.

When someone asks why you're not devastated about your child going off to college, remind them that you're filled with pride and excitement. You've spent years helping them grow into the independent, capable person they are today, and now it's their time to shine. Watching them step into this new chapter, pursue their dreams, and become an amazing adult is something to celebrate! It's not about sadness but embracing the joy of seeing your child flourish and knowing you've equipped them to take on the world. You're excited for them and the new journey you're both starting.

If your friend tries to pull you into their sadness, or make you feel guilty for not being a hot mess, simply thank them for the concern and whip out one of these pre-written responses:

- "I'm so proud of them for reaching this point—it feels like the start of an exciting new chapter for both of us."

- "Of course, I'll miss them, but I'm more focused on celebrating their independence."

- "I'm genuinely happy for them—and for me! It's a big change; I'm focusing on all the positives this brings."

- "I'm saving my tears for when they move back home after college with all their laundry!"

- "Why should I be sad? I shed tears of joy looking at my grocery bill; it's half of what it used to be!"

#88

Expect a unique experience for your child, not a carbon copy of your own college experience.

Remember that your child's college journey will be uniquely theirs, not a repeat of your own. It's easy to fall into the trap of projecting your college experience onto them, but their path will be shaped by their personality, interests, and the world they're growing up in. While you might have had unforgettable moments on campus, don't use those memories as a template for what your child should experience. Their college years will have different challenges, opportunities, and even new social dynamics. Instead of reliving your glory days through them, try embracing their individuality's excitement. Support their choices, even if they differ from yours. They might choose a major you never considered or get involved in activities that weren't part of your college scene. That's okay! What's important is that they feel empowered to create their own story. Let them take ownership of their experience, and don't impose your expectations. Their journey is a fresh chapter filled with their own dreams and discoveries. Celebrate that they are making it their own and give them the freedom to learn and grow in ways that are right for them.

"When I stopped comparing my son's college experience to my own, we actually grew closer."

#89

You may grow closer to your child during the college years.

If you approach this college transition with the right mindset, it might bring you closer to your child. As they navigate their new independence, they'll go through a range of emotions, and having a supportive, understanding parent to talk to can make all the difference. Instead of hovering, try being a steady source of encouragement and advice when they reach out. Giving them the space to grow while still being available when needed shows them that you trust their judgment. This creates a stronger bond built on mutual respect and understanding. College can be a time of new challenges, and when your child realizes that they can turn to you for guidance without fear of judgment, they may open up in ways they haven't before. Be there to listen but also give them the room to figure things out on their own. When you're not trying to control every decision, you'll see them start to appreciate your wisdom and feel more comfortable sharing their successes and struggles. This new dynamic can deepen your relationship and foster a more mature, supportive connection as they continue to grow.

"The first year I felt like my relationship with my daughter was never going to be the same... in a bad way. And, yes, it was rough, but we kept talking and giving each other space. By the time she graduated, we had a better, although different, relationship. I guess what I'm trying to say is, be patient and don't put too much pressure on either of you."

#90

Don't drink yourself silly.

While it's natural to want to unwind and cope with the emotional rollercoaster of your child leaving for college, drowning your sorrows in alcohol won't help. It may offer temporary relief, but it won't fill your emotional gap. Instead of turning to excessive drinking, try healthier ways to manage the transition—like journaling, exercising, or chatting with a close friend. Remember, this is a time of growth for both you and your child. By taking care of yourself in a balanced way, you'll be in a better mindset to navigate this new chapter. Overindulging can cloud your ability to think clearly, and you don't want to miss out on the meaningful opportunities that come with this time of change. Instead, focus on finding new routines, passions, and ways to reenergize. It's important to embrace change with a clear head so you can make the most of this new phase in life, both for yourself and your ongoing relationship with your child.

"My son came home for a surprise one weekend, took one look at my recycling bin and said, 'And, I thought I drank a lot!' That was all it took for me to realize my daily habit of wine with dinner had gotten out of control. I vowed to become a better role model for my son... and myself."

#91

Realize you will have your own adjustment period.

As your child transitions to college, it's easy to focus entirely on their new chapter and forget to check in with your own well-being. This is a significant adjustment for you, too—a time of change, mixed emotions, and rediscovery. After years as a primary caregiver, you may suddenly find yourself with more space, fewer routines, and a sense of uncertainty about how to fill your time. That's perfectly normal. This transition is an opportunity to nurture your own growth, rediscover interests, and focus on personal goals or hobbies you may have set aside. Whether it's exploring new passions, pampering yourself with small treats, or simply allowing yourself time to reflect, this is your moment to invest in your happiness and well-being. Don't feel guilty for prioritizing yourself—embrace it as a healthy and necessary part of this new phase. Taking care of your mental and emotional health helps you feel balanced and sets an example for your child about the importance of self-care. Like them, you're stepping into a new chapter, and it's okay to take it slow. Over time, you'll find your rhythm again, and this milestone will bring fresh purpose and freedom to your own life.

"I told everyone that I joined a volleyball team because my daughter left for college. Someone said to me, 'Shouldn't you do something for yourself, not because of your child?' That was pretty brutal, but, necessary. I hadn't thought about it that way."

#92

If you have other children at home, don't smother them because you miss the other one.

It's natural to feel a bit of emptiness when one child leaves for college, but it's important not to project that onto your other children. They still need your attention, love, and space to grow in their own way. Just because one child has moved on to the next chapter doesn't mean your relationship with your other kids should change in response. Give them the chance to thrive without feeling like they must fill the gap left behind. Instead of smothering them out of your own feelings of loss, let them explore their independence too. You might be surprised at how much they'll grow when they sense your trust and support, not your anxiety or over-protection. Keep the balance—allow your younger children the freedom to develop their own path, just as you did with their siblings—they deserve it. Plus, as you embrace your role as a parent to multiple children, you're teaching them valuable lessons about resilience, flexibility, and emotional strength. Give them the space to flourish and remember that each child's journey is unique.

"Once our first child left for college, I turned all my attention to his sister, who got overwhelmed with the excessive attention to the point she finally told me I needed to back off and give her some space."

#93

---

*The separation will become not only tolerable
but exciting as well.*

As your child heads off to college, the initial separation may feel overwhelming, but with time, you'll find that it becomes not only tolerable, but exciting. Watching your child take steps toward independence is a milestone, and feeling a mix of emotions is natural. However, don't fall into the trap of guilt. This is exactly what you've been working toward, raising a confident, capable individual who's now ready to embrace new experiences. Instead of focusing on the void they leave behind, embrace the opportunity to rediscover your own passions, routines, and even relationships that may have taken a backseat while you were in full parenting mode. This is a time for both of you to grow. Your child is learning to stand on their own two feet, and you are learning to embrace your evolving role. There's no need for guilt, only pride in how far they've come. Separation can be a moment of personal growth for both of you, with the added benefit of building a new and stronger relationship as they move forward in life. It's all part of the beautiful, bittersweet parenting journey.

"Because our son was in college across the country, he didn't come home often. We had a lot of time to settle into a new routine, but the distance made it that much more special when he did come home."

#94

The first year will fly by, trust me!

The first year of your child's college journey will feel like a blur—trust me on this one! It might seem like it's dragging on in the beginning as you adjust to the change, but before you know it, you'll be celebrating their first holiday break, and they'll be coming home with stories of college life. As much as you focus on how different everything feels, this first year will pass in the blink of an eye. It's important to savor the little moments—those quick check-ins, the surprise texts, and even the quiet spaces where you get to breathe. The initial transition can feel overwhelming, but soon enough, your child will have found their rhythm, and you'll have found a new sense of balance. So, hang in there, take a deep breath, and enjoy the ride. It'll go faster than you think!

"I don't know what I was so worried about. They leave, and before you know it, it's parents' weekend, then Thanksgiving, then winter break (which is really long), then spring break, then they're home. Seriously, you blink and the first year is gone."

#95

Now is a wonderful time to reconnect with your partner and friends, but not just to commiserate.

Now that your child is off to college, it's the perfect time to reconnect with your partner and friends—but don't just use this as an opportunity to commiserate about the empty seat at the dinner table. Instead, embrace the chance to rediscover what you love about your relationships. Take a fresh look at your partnership and explore ways to rekindle that connection. You've spent years focused on parenting, so now is a wonderful time to prioritize each other again—whether that means enjoying quiet evenings, tackling a new hobby together, or simply having deeper conversations without the distractions of family life. Similarly, reconnecting with friends can provide much-needed support and camaraderie. This isn't about feeling sorry for yourself, but rather about celebrating the freedom and growth that comes with this new chapter.

> *"Warning! Talk about reconnecting... while my daughter was away, I reconnected with an old flame, and we began seeing each other again. While I was super excited for them to meet, my daughter was less than thrilled. My advice for any single parent is to really focus on your child during school break, then make introductions to new 'special friends' slowly."*

#96

Find new ways to communicate with your child.

The days of casual conversations at the dinner table or texting throughout the day will become less frequent, but that doesn't mean the connection has to fade. Start by discussing what communication looks like now for both of you—whether it's a weekly phone call, a set time to FaceTime, or sending messages or photos through text or apps. Be open to their preferences and respect their growing independence while also establishing moments for you to check in on each other. You can also surprise them with care packages or handwritten notes that show you're thinking of them and use social media to share snippets of your life that can spark new conversations. Get creative—share memes, quotes, or interesting things you discover. Try keeping it light, fun, and positive, but don't shy away from having deeper, more thoughtful conversations when the time is right. The goal is to nurture the connection you've always had while respecting their need to spread their wings. Be flexible and patient with yourself and them as you navigate this new dynamic but always remember that the lines of communication can remain strong with a little effort and creativity.

"My son stopped answering his phone and I thought something was wrong. He told me that now that he's in college, he would prefer me to send text messages. With his schedule, it was not always convenient to pick up. We simply had to set new ground rules."

#97

Don't wallow in reminiscing.

As tempting as it may be to spend hours reminiscing about the "good old days" when your child was still at home, try not to get stuck in the past. Yes, it's natural to feel a sense of loss as they venture off into the next chapter of their life, but dwelling on it too long can keep you from embracing the exciting new stage ahead. Your child is growing and evolving, and so should you. Instead of fixating on what was, focus on what is and what's coming next. Think about the fresh opportunities this new phase offers—for you and for them. This is a great time to invest in your own passions, hobbies, and friendships. It's a season of growth for both you and your child, and your emotional energy is better spent looking forward, not back. Celebrate the milestones, and acknowledge your feelings, but also remember that life is full of change, and each new step brings its own set of possibilities. By keeping your mindset focused forward, you'll be supporting your child and embracing the positive changes that come with this transition.

"I had to accept that the child who left for college would be different when they came home. Instead of missing what used to be, I started saying I was getting the 'new and improved' version of my son. This small shift in perspective helped me to stop looking back."

#98

Find a new focus to fill this gap in your life and give you something meaningful to focus on.

As your child heads off to college, it's natural to feel a void in your life, but this transition is also a perfect opportunity to rediscover joy and purpose. Think of it as a chance to explore personal passions that may have taken a backseat over the years. Whether it's starting a new hobby, pursuing a long-forgotten interest, or volunteering for a cause you care about, this is your time to focus on what excites and fulfills you. Consider starting a creative project, taking a class, or diving into something that sparks curiosity and growth. By finding something meaningful to focus on, you not only fill the gap left by your child's departure but also reclaim a sense of personal achievement and energy. This shift isn't just about staying busy—it's about embracing the freedom to pursue what makes you happy and sharing that excitement when your child comes home. Show them that growth doesn't stop at any stage of life. Investing in yourself enriches your life and serves as a reminder that this new chapter is an opportunity for both you and your child to thrive. You've earned this time—make it positive, meaningful, and uniquely yours!

"A friend suggested that I sign up for something that started over the summer, so I would already be engaged when my daughter went off to school. This way, I was less likely to bail on the commitment, and I had something to look forward to. I have to admit, it was a great suggestion. I joined a weekly bocce ball league and everyone was so supportive."

#99

Don't overwhelm yourself by thinking about the future.

It's easy to get caught up in worrying about what comes next, especially when your child is stepping into a new chapter of their life. But don't let yourself become overwhelmed by the unknowns. The future can feel huge and unpredictable, and it's natural to want to plan, but the truth is, you can only control so much. Take it one day at a time and remember that each moment your child experiences will help shape them into the person they're meant to be. Worrying about what's ahead won't help them or you—it just takes away from the present. Trust that they're learning and growing as they need to and that you've done your part to prepare them. Focus on being there when they need you and enjoy the moments you have now. When you allow yourself to be present, you'll find it easier to support your child and handle whatever comes up next without getting bogged down by worry. The future will unfold, as it always does, one step at a time.

"My son was only a month into his freshman year, and I was already bugging him if he had visited the career development center. I was more nervous about him graduating than getting through his first year. My husband reined me in and said, 'Just breathe... the future comes one step at a time.' Just breathe became my mantra when I was feeling anxious."

#100

While you are proud of your child, be proud of yourself too!

As your child steps into this exciting new chapter, it's easy to focus all your pride on them, but don't forget to celebrate yourself too! You've put in years of love, guidance, and hard work to help them get to this point, and that's something to be proud of. This is as much your achievement as it is theirs. You've navigated the ups and downs of parenting, made sacrifices, and set them up for success, and now you're seeing the results. Take a moment to appreciate all you've done. This transition isn't just about them growing up—it's about your growth too. So, hold your head up high and give yourself the credit you deserve. You've helped launch someone into the world, and that's a huge accomplishment! Embrace this moment of pride and gratitude for both you and your child. You've earned it.

> *"I had a few friends who were also sending their kids off to college at the same time we were. Once the kids were gone, we threw a 'parental graduation' party. We sat around and told stories about raising our kids, the mistakes, the times we went over and above, the sacrifices we made and the times we totally embarrassed them. We gave ourselves one heck of a party, celebrating our accomplishments, and shared plans for our newfound free time."*

What's Next?

Congratulations on completing this book filled with wisdom from real people! As you've journeyed through the pages, you've discovered the profound truth encapsulated in the quote:

Wisdom is the reward of experience and should be shared.

Your role as the bearer of this wisdom doesn't end here. Your journey is just beginning. Embrace the opportunity to continue sharing wisdom and to uplift and inspire others on their paths. Let this remind us that we should not hoard wisdom but generously share it with those in need.

So, my friend, as you close this book, carry its lessons forward. And remember, your experiences and life lessons are your wisdom. They are invaluable treasures waiting to be shared with the world. Let's continue to learn from one another, grow, and spread positive energy and wisdom wherever we go.

About the Author

Jen Fort is a writer, coach, and natural-born encourager who believes the right words at the right time can be a lifeline. She created the Wisdom & Warnings series to capture real advice from real people—because no one gets through life's biggest transitions without a little help. *Let Them Fly* was born from Jen's personal journey—transitioning from single parent to witnessing both of her children spread their wings and leave the nest.

Visit www.iamjenfort.com to:

- Share your favorite nuggets of wisdom and perhaps have your wisdom included in future books.

- Receive free resource suggestions.

- Be the first to know about upcoming Wisdom & Warnings book releases.

- Find out how you can further benefit from Jen's life mission to encourage and share life's lessons!